HOT TO GO

First published in 2025 by OH
An Imprint of HEADLINE PUBLISHING GROUP LIMITED

1

Disclaimer:
This book has not been licensed, approved, sponsored, or endorsed by Chappell Roan.

Chappell Roan is a registered trademark owned by Kayleigh Rose Amstutz.

Cataloguing in Publication Data is available from the British Library

ISBN 978-1-03543-175-5

Compiled and written by: Malcolm Croft
Editorial: Saneaah Muhammad
Designed and typeset in Avenir LT Std by: Stephen Cary
Project manager: Russell Porter
Production: Arlene Lestrade
Printed and bound in Dubai

Headline's policy is to use papers that are natural, renewable and recyclable products and made from wood grown in well-managed forests and other controlled sources. The logging and manufacturing processes are expected to conform to the environmental regulations of the country of origin.

HEADLINE PUBLISHING GROUP LIMITED
An Hachette UK Company
Carmelite House, 50 Victoria Embankment, London EC4Y 0DZ

The authorised representative in the EEA is Hachette Ireland, 8 Castlecourt Centre, Dublin 15, D15 XTP3, Ireland (email: info@hbgi.ie)

www.headline.co.uk www.hachette.co.uk

HOT TO GO

THE LITTLE GUIDE TO CHAPPELL ROAN

UNOFFICIAL AND UNAUTHORIZED

CONTENTS

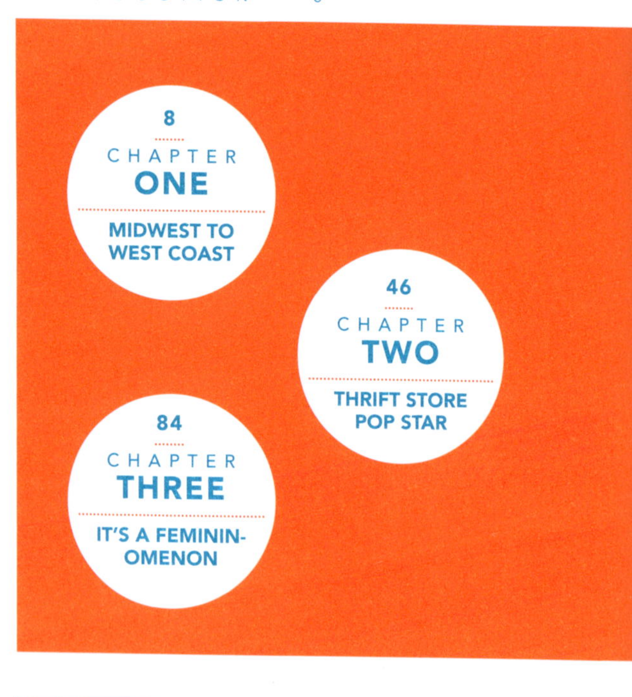

INTRODUCTION

Welcome to the wild and wonderful world of Chappell Roan. And, make no mistake, it is a world that belongs to Princess Chappell right now. The rest of us are merely her adoring subjects.

Since her dramatic bursting into the world at large in 2023 – though, obvs, she's been a star in the making since she signed her first record deal in 2015 – Chappell has been all anyone has talked about, transforming herself from a bored belt barista, barely existing, into a beautiful social butterfly. Now, she is a shining, sparkly symbol of self-discovery and a million-selling, multiple Grammy-nominated and one-time Grammy winner (so far!) pop icon whose music is a beaming beacon of hope for feminism, queer rights and individual empowerment in America's divided society. In a nutshell: Chappell Roan is a femininomenon.

After more than a few false starts, and after relocating from the backwater town of

Willard, Missouri to the bright lights of Los Angeles, California, Chappell finally released *The Rise and Fall of a Midwest Princess*, a magnificently manicured masterpiece studded with rhinestone campness, unfiltered joy, flamboyant glitz and more anthemic bangers than you can shake a (bright red) lipstick at. It's an album that defines, and defies, the age we live in. Not bad for a debut.

Witty, wise and wonderfully refreshing, just like Chappell, this tiny tome celebrates all that is fantastic about your favourite artist's favourite artist, as told by the Midwest Princess herself through her earliest and most iconic interviews. If you're looking for the voice of her generation, stop searching, because it's right here.

Only one question remains: Are you ready for it, bitches?

CHAPTER ONE

MIDWEST TO WEST COAST

Kayleigh Rose Amstutz's transformation from "moody" Missouri teen to Chappell Roan, the rhinestone-rockin' drag-pop queen of California, is a decade-long journey of self-discovery… and a whole lot of vajazzling.

Though, with great fame comes some side-effects, all of which Chappell is ploughing through.

Welcome to the show…

If a five-year-old could draw a pop star, it would be me.

Chappell, on being the ultimate pop star, *Rolling Stone*, October 27, 2022

“Don’t call me baby, and don’t call me Kayleigh.”

The line that Chappell opens her shows with – the phrase ends with “You only get to call me one thing… I am the Midwest Princess!”

Chappell Roan, Kayleigh’s stage name and drag-pop persona, is inspired by her beloved, late grandfather, Dennis Chappell, and his favourite song, “The Strawberry Roan”, a classic American cowboy song written by Curley Fletcher in 1915. A roan, in case you didn’t know, is the term used to describe a horse that has a coat that is one solid colour mixed with white hairs across its body.

I grew up on Christian rock. And I will say, with my whole chest, it's the worst music I've ever heard.

Chappell, on her opinion of religious rock'n'roll, *The Line of Best Fit*, June 22, 2023

“

I don’t identify with the Christian Church anymore, but I’m really glad that I was part of that community because I understand them. I understand that perspective. I know where they’re coming from. I have a different understanding when it comes to really confusing things that most people are like, ‘What the fuck?’

”

Chappell, on how her religious upbringing shaped her, *Vanity Fair*, September 18, 2023

“

I got on TikTok to show my personality and how I love to thrift and have style and do makeup. And when I saw that people were not only connecting to the music but this aesthetic I was building of this DIY pop girl, I was like ‘Oh, I have more to play with here than just music. I have a whole world that I can build.’ I just filled that out and used drag and burlesque as stakeholders.

”

Chappell, on the genesis behind the creation of Chappell Roan as a drag queen, *Dork*, December 21, 2023

At the age of 12, when Chappell was in eighth grade, she entered a school talent contest and won. It was the first time she ever sang and played the piano in public.

Soon after, she began posting covers on YouTube. In 2014, Chappell uploaded her first original song, "Die Young", a doom-laden, heartbreak ballad. It led her to be signed by Atlantic Records in 2015, aged just 17.

It was then that she changed her stage name to Chappell Roan.

Fame is like going through puberty. I have all these new emotions and I'm really confused. It's how it felt to be 12.

Chappell, on the process and emotions of fame, *The Guardian*, September 20, 2024

Chappell is so extravagant... and my personality is a sliver of that.

Chappell, on the differences between Chappell and Kayleigh, *Afterglow*, September 18, 2023

I wanted to wear weird, fun clothes, and I felt like I couldn't do that with 'Die Young'. It just felt too dark. So I had to change my music, because it was not sustainable. I wanted to push myself – I wanted to be bold and say things that might be a little edgy. I come from a super conservative area where I wouldn't even wear the things that I wear in L.A. here in public. So I decided I'm just going to be everything that I am in L.A., in my music.

Chappell, on her transformation from moody Missouri teen to cool Californian, *Headliner*, April 2021

Every big thing that happens to someone's career happened in like five months for me. It's crazy because things that I never thought would happen, happened times ten.

Chappell, on her overwhelming rise to global fame, *Teen Vogue*, November 10, 2024

I had to hit rock bottom. I got dropped and ended a four-and-a-half-year relationship. I lost all my money and had to move back in with my parents. This was 2020 and I was working at a drive-through. I was like, 'Oh my dear God, this is it, but I'm gonna give it one last hurrah.' And that is how I found myself – out of necessity. A lot of my outfits were thrifted and I had to learn how to do my own drag makeup. If I wanted to do a photo shoot, I had to ask my friends to help me. Thank God, I didn't give up. But I was very, very close.

Chappell, on the turning point when she realized who she was as an artist, *NME*, June 21, 2023

I felt so miserable for my whole childhood. All my parents could do was try their best. But I can't go my whole life hating my parents for not knowing how to handle a really, really sick child. I was just miserable. Going to therapy together saved us.

Chappell, on moving back to Missouri, aged 22, and starting therapy with her parents in order to heal, *Rolling Stone*, September 10, 2024

“

Honestly, picking my name was the hardest part out of it all because you're stuck with it once you pick it. I went through – I'm not kidding – thousands of names, and I always kept coming back to Chappell because it's a family name. And I found out I couldn't just be 'Chappell,' that's what I originally had wanted, so I picked Chappell Roan.

”

Chappell, on choosing her pop persona moniker Chappell Roan, *Unclear*, December 10, 2017

It was completely eye-opening and changed my direction from that point on. I danced my ass off and I didn't care; it was one of the most fun nights ever… there were go-go dancers on the table, and I walked in and it was the most spiritual experience. I just felt overwhelmed with complete love and acceptance.

”

Chappell, on discovering her true self after visiting iconic L.A. gay bar The Abbey for the first time, *Headliner*, April 2021

It feels like a different person, honestly. It just reminds me – wow, I have come so far. That was me when I was a very moody, angry teen. Every time I hear 'Die Young' or when someone brings it up, I'm like, 'I still don't even know how I wrote it', because I don't even think I understood what it was about when I wrote it, fully.

Chappell, on feeling estranged from her younger self and her old songs, *Headliner*, April 2021

I originally started doing music because I wanted to get my foot in the door for acting, and then I moved to Los Angeles, and I was like, 'Fuck that.'

Chappell, on wanting to be an actor originally, *Interview*, August 19, 2024

Classic Disney movies played such a huge role in my love for music. I would watch *Pocahontas* or Ariel and be obsessed with every song in the movie.

”

Chappell, on her earliest influences and inspirations, idreamofvinyl.com, May 7, 2020

"My whole life has changed. Everything that I really love to do now comes with baggage. If I want to go thrifting, I have to book security and prepare myself that this is not going to be normal. Going to the park, Pilates, yoga – how do I do this in a safe way where I'm not going to be stalked or harassed?"

Chappell, on the negative elements of being a celebrity, *The Guardian*, September 20, 2024

1. "Die Young"
2. "Good Hurt"
3. "Meantime"
4. "Sugar High"
5. "Bad For You"

In 2017, Chappell released her debut EP, *School Nights*.

The five-song collection is fairly folky and was released on September 22*– the one-year anniversary of her grandfather Dennis Chappell's passing; an unplanned, but serendipitous, coincidence.

Another eight tracks were recorded for the EP, but scrapped.

* *If you listen closely, you can hear the sound of a clock in every song.*

“It feels so good to prove Atlantic Records wrong because they weren’t just a little wrong. They were really, really, really wrong. To know that my gut instinct was right is the best feeling in the world. Purposeful revenge does not feel good, but revenge by accident feels awesome.”

Chappell, on being a global success for Island Records after being dropped by Atlantic Records in 2020 for her "underwhelming music", *Rolling Stone*, September 10, 2024

It was super hard to adapt from a small rural town to Los Angeles and New York. I had never seen a skyscraper! We're so far away from the ocean back home, even. I was shocked... for three years straight!

Chappell, on touring out of her home state for the first time as a teenager to promote her first EP, *Headliner*, April 2021

My name is Chappell Roan. I'm 19. I'm from Springfield, Missouri and I still live there. I would say my music is pop, but it's got like a darker twist to it and more of a haunting type deal. I don't know, it's so hard to explain it 'cause it's a lot of different things.

”

Chappell, trying to define Chappell Roan and her music, *Unclear*, December 10, 2017

Stevie Nicks and Karen Carpenter are my main vocal influences. When I was younger I would try to mimic their voices. Lady Gaga and Beyoncé really inspire me with their stage presence. They are both so confident and really own the stage and connect with the crowd so well. I hope to be like them one day. Frida Kahlo is my favourite artist. I love the darkness and vulnerability of her paintings.

”

Chappell, on her creative inspirations, *Anchr Magazine*, April 2, 2018

All of a sudden I realized I could truly be any way I wanted to be, and no one would bat an eye. It was so different from home, where I always had such a hard time being myself and felt like I'd be judged for being different or being creative. I just felt overwhelmed with complete love and acceptance, and from then on I started writing songs as the real me.

Chappell, on the fun night out at iconic gay bar The Abbey in L.A. that altered her perspective on being an artist, Bringin' It Backwards podcast, September 14, 2022

I was very suicidal for years, very mentally ill, and not medicated, because that's just not a part of Midwest culture. It's not: 'Maybe we should get you a psychiatrist.' It's: 'You need God. You need to pray about that.'

Chappell, on conservative and repressed Midwest culture, *The Guardian*, September 20, 2024

I was 17 when I got signed, and it just felt like a whirlwind. And I felt kind of lost and it was very overwhelming. But it was the best learning experience.

Chappell, on signing her first record deal with Atlantic Records in 2015, *Headliner*, April 2021

My mom getting me my first CD – P!nk's *Missundaztood*. I listened to it all the time.

”

Chappell, on her first musical memory, *Anchr Magazine*, April 2, 2018

> “I loved it when I wore the prosthetic pig nose. That felt very daring and was kind of scary, in a fun way.”

Chappell, on her now-famous pig nose outfit, worn at the Universal Music Group's 66th Grammy Awards After Party celebration, *Atwood Magazine*, August 26, 2024

I thought I was gonna get married right out of high school, at 18 or 19, and I thought I was gonna have a baby by 23. I tried to fit myself into that mould and it didn't work. It left me with a really interesting relationship with the Midwest.

Chappell, on her expected life path not turning out the way everyone else expected, *Polyester*, October 26, 2024

The Midwest remains a very big part of who I am. It's where I grew up and I do love certain parts of it – the peace, growing up in a trailer park, four wheeling, the farm and bonfires. I love it even more now because I can reflect on it all like 'Oh, my God, this is so camp.'

Chappell, on the pleasures and positives of her Midwest upbringing, *Polyester*, October 26, 2024

I was a teenager at an incredible time; Lorde had just dropped *Pure Heroine*, Lana had just dropped *Born To Die*, Kesha was in full swing and Gaga had come out with *The Fame Monster*. Rihanna had *Rated R* and *Teenage Dream* and Drake was just starting to gain momentum. I was obsessed with it all.

Chappell, on her musical inspirations and influences as a teenager, *The Line of Best Fit*, June 22, 2023

I had no idea what was going on and neither did my parents or my parents' friends. It was so messy. I felt very unprepared. I didn't know the consequences of how much I had to sacrifice. I didn't do my senior year. I didn't go to prom. I didn't go to graduation. I missed a lot of what would have been the end of my childhood to do this job.

”

Chappell, on the sacrifices of signing a record deal at age 17, *Rolling Stone*, October 27, 2022

I couldn't write pop songs when I was depressed on a farm in Missouri. I just needed to get out of there to finish the rest of the songs that needed to be written. I was working the drive-through and I would just think of little song melodies and write on my Notes app. And that's kind of how I kept the flame going.

Chappell, on returning to Los Angeles (for one final shot) after the pandemic ended in order to finish the album she started in 2020 with producer Daniel Nigro, *Vanity Fair*, September 18, 2023

Please – don't call me Kayleigh.

Chappell, in an Instagram message to her "super fans" who use her real name when they shouldn't, August 23, 2024

I remember them calling me and being like: 'You don't even play guitar'. I was so fucking mad. I said: 'Ariana Grande has a guitar solo in "Dangerous Woman" and she doesn't touch a guitar'. It felt like a cop-out from the label, and it was such a pivot from where I'd been in the past, musically. It was a hard song to grow into, because the label made me feel stupid. I thought they were right for a while.

Chappell, on the "Pink Pony Club" guitar solo being used as the reason Atlantic Records dropped her in 2020, interview with Charlie Duncan, Pink News, July 22, 2023

At the very beginning, I was doing a lot of dark synth pop. It was ballady, witchy and melodramatic. I listened to Lana del Rey, Lorde and Ellie Goulding my entire high school.

Chappell, on her sound when signed to Atlantic Records in 2015, Pop Crave, February 15, 2023

CHAPTER TWO

THRIFT STORE POP STAR

Since her dramatic crossbow-wielding arrival on the world stage, Chappell has been described as "the future of pop".

Long before that, however, Chappell took her career by the horns and manufactured and manifested her own DIY destiny, never once compromising on her vision.

As a result, Ms Roan has redefined what it means to be a pop star in the 21st century. If the future belongs to Chappell, then it starts right here, right now...

I just wanted a girl who was free and unapologetically herself. I wanted to create concerts where people could dress up and have a blast. I just wanted to be a drag queen.

Chappell, on why she chose the art of drag as the primary inspiration for her vision for Chappell Roan, *Dork*, December 21, 2023

Drag is like a spa for my soul.

”

Chappell, on her love for drag, *The Guardian*, September 20, 2024

> "The raunchiness of the music as Chappell Roan is really liberating for me, because I have such a difficult time – as Kayleigh – with sex. I have a hard time watching sex scenes or flirting with people, I get really uncomfortable with hyper sexual things. But as the drag queen that I play, Chappell, she's not like that – she is very confident and comfortable singing about those things."

Chappell, on the raunchiness of her music and her sexuality as Chappell, *Polyester*, October 26, 2024

“

As a kid, I thought being gay was a choice. I'm still working through internal homophobia. When it's ingrained in you, it's in your blood. I'm still working it out. Now I've evolved, I see how important it is to actually create safe spaces the best I can. We need that. I need that.

”

Chappell, on religious indoctrination and creating a safe, inclusive space for gay people at her shows, *PinkNews*, July 22, 2023

“

If I could redo all of this, I would be Daft Punk.* Ten thousand per cent.

”

Chappell, on having more privacy, *Paper*, June 4, 2024

** Daft Punk hid their faces under masks to retain a level of privacy.*

When I'm on stage, when I'm performing, when I'm in drag, when I'm at a work event, when I'm doing press… I am at work. Any other circumstance, I am not in work mode. I am clocked out. I don't agree with the notion that I owe a mutual exchange of energy, time, or attention to people I do not know, do not trust, or who creep me out – just because they're expressing admiration.

Chappell, on creating boundaries between Chappell, her character, and Kayleigh, the person, Instagram, August 23, 2024

"If I saw myself now when I was 16 I would be like no way, there's no way I would do that! Let myself write a song that's about being a hot person and being a cheerleader, I'm too serious for that."

Chappell, on the seriousness of her formative sound when signed to Atlantic Records in 2014, Crucial Rhythm, September 12, 2023

“

My songs are a vessel to the LGBTQ+ community and they have allowed me to be in a room with all these queer people who are experiencing joy – and the songs have been a way for me to find those things in myself.

”

Chappell, on her songs being paths to finding a connection with the gay community, The Forty-Five, January 18, 2024

Prepare to be silly. Don't take it so seriously. I find myself with music when I listen to something brand new. I'm super hypercritical of it. Give it a chance, it's going to feel silly. Allow yourself to feel silly and fun.

”

Chappell, on her artistic process and how to prepare to listen to *The Rise and Fall of a Midwest Princess*, Crucial Rhythm, September 12, 2023

Everywhere I play there's always just one random boy who doesn't want to be there. They're the ones I pick on the whole time. I called some guy out last night and I was like, 'What's your name?' He was like, 'Seth,' and I was like, 'Are you good at dancing?' And he was like, 'No.' I was like, 'Well, we are about to teach you "HOT TO GO!"' And I was like, 'You fucked with the wrong pop star.'

Chappell, on fans who don't quite dig all the drag and themes at her live shows, *Salt Lake*, August 29, 2024

I'm not the character of Chappell Roan in real life.

Chappell, on differentiating herself from her drag persona, *Teen Vogue*, March 9, 2023

I don't like writing music. It's very emotional and ridiculously hard for me. The hardest song to write emotionally was 'Meantime' because at the time I was in this relationship and I felt like I couldn't give everything to them. So I was basically saying, 'Can I love you in the meantime while I figure myself out?'

99

Chappell, on one of her earliest compositions, "Meantime", and the difficulty of writing pop music, *Unclear*, December 10, 2017

When I hit 24, that's when I started liking myself enough to become this drag version of myself.

”

Chappell, on the age she started feeling comfortable within herself, *The Line of Best Fit*, June 22, 2023

“

I’m very proud of myself. I’m proud that I kept going through all of the part-time jobs, through being dropped by a label, through all the breakups, through all the times my bank account was nearly empty. I’m very grateful that I kept going, and it feels very good, it feels very right.

”

Chappell, on being proud of herself for making her dreams come true through sheer persistence, *Salt Lake*, August 29, 2024

I'm delving into this version of myself I never allowed myself to be, which is like this sparkly, tacky, loud, obnoxious version. It's pretty much the opposite of what I was taught to be. Growing up I had this little girl trapped inside me that never got to express herself the way she dreamed of – that just kind of unfolded into this project.

Chappell, on allowing herself to explore her individuality, BroadwayWorld, September 27, 2023

I've been poor, so I know I can be happy and poor. Not having money doesn't scare me.

Chappell, on being rich without money, The Comment Section with Drew Afualo podcast, July 14, 2024

All my dreams came true. This is it, I don't need anything else. I'm having a blast.

Chappell, on her dreams coming true, *Salt Lake*, August 29, 2024

If it's not bold, if it's not ruffling feathers, what's the point?

”

Chappell, on her music serving a purpose, *The Guardian*, December 29, 2023

My music used to be very dark, like piano ballad pop, very Lorde, Lana-esque. I was just a teenager who was really depressed and sad and I think it just really reflected that. What changed was that I moved to California. My eyes were opened to so many new things and so many fun people. I was doing things that I never thought I was able to do. I thought 'the new sound' just reflected what was genuinely going on with my life.

Chappell, on her transformation from moody Missouri teen to cool Californian, Rising Artists, September 29, 2023

I am not trying to be a chic bitch. I love the chic bitches, but I am not trying to be like that. Nothing turns me off more than frickin' luxury brands.

Chappell, on wearing high-end fashion – Chappell loves a good thriftin'! *Paper*, June 4, 2024.

Vajazzling is really therapeutic for me.

Chappell, on vajazzling, "a very drag queen thing", The Forty-Five, January 18, 2024

I ask myself 'What would be the funniest thing to perform live?' That's how I write.

Chappell, on her unique songwriting process, *The Guardian*, September 20, 2024

Chappell's favourite drag queen is Sasha Colby. In 2012, Colby won the Miss Continental competition, one of the most prestigious drag queen pageants in the world, and, in 2023, she was crowned the winner of the 15th season of RuPaul's Drag Race and became America's "Next Drag Superstar".

After learning that she was Chappell's favourite drag queen, Colby told *EW*, in July 2024: "Drag has always been a mirror of pop culture. Since *Drag Race*, we are pop, the tastemakers, and pop girlies look to us for inspiration – much like Chappell Roan! All I can say is, goddess sees goddess, you know? Greatness sees greatness! Your favourite artist's favourite artist, baby!"

I wear grey and black IRL because I can't handle the shit that I wear onstage.

”

Chappell, on being as plainly dressed as possible when not performing as Chappell Roan, *Rolling Stone*, September 10, 2024

Miley Cyrus sacrificed herself for us all with the foam finger. 2013, that was a crazy fucking year. That was when I was 15 and so that was like very, very instrumental to my knowledge of pop culture. I was just like, 'Holy shit, what is going on?'

Chappell, on 2013, the year that belonged to Miley Cyrus, BroadwayWorld, September 27, 2023

It's been a decade. This has been ten years of perfecting a craft.

”

Chappell, on her 10-year journey to becoming an overnight sensation, *Five Cent Sound*, November 3, 2023

Pop music was shining a light on a part of myself that I was trying to dim. But it was always deep down inside. I was just scared to be that version of myself – it seemed too big and loud.

Chappell, on her love and passion for pop music, *DIY*, July 28, 2023

It's been four years in the making. She's ready – she's like, 'Get me out, it's time.' I've taken my time with it. I did not cut corners. I respected the art and let it breathe. And it's also just, like, we need the party right now. The world is on fire, so let's just party.

Chappell, on the extended birthing of debut album *The Rise and Fall of a Midwest Princess, NME,* June 21, 2023

You can't solidify an identity after only a year without looking inauthentic. It takes fucking years. Being Chappell Roan is based on two things: Does it give me butterflies? And is it a 100 per cent yes? If it's not a yes, it's a no. You can't fucking compromise.

Chappell, on the process of creating Chappell Roan and the certainty of the identity, *DIY*, July 28, 2023

I was 17 and I thought I was gonna win a Grammy. It's funny, because, when you sign to a label, that's when the real work begins.

Chappell, on her dreams when she started out in the music industry, *The Guardian*, December 29, 2023

Live Shows

Every single live show of Chappell's is themed after a song from the album *The Rise and Fall of a Midwest Princess* (2023).

Attendees of the live concert shows are encouraged to dress to theme as much as possible. Chappell's favourite theme was "Angels and Devils", which she did for all her Halloween shows in October 2024 – she had massive angel wings! – but other themes include: "Pink Pony Club" (pink cowgirl), "Midwest Princess" (camouflage and pink), "My Kink is Karma" (black and red) and several more.

“

'Good Luck, Babe!' does not warrant me coming out with a weapon on fire, but I was like, I have to do it. This is what I really would have wanted as my 11-year-old boy version of myself.

”

Chappell, on that now-iconic September 2024 MTV VMA performance of "Good Luck, Babe!", and Chappell's medieval-inspired theme onstage (dressed as a knight, shooting a fiery arrow with a crossbow, setting a castle on fire and wielding swords), *The Guardian*, September 20, 2024

** This performance was Chappell's first big awards show. What a first impression!*

> “I got the idea of drag queens from Orville Peck at his show in 2018 at the Troubadour in West Hollywood. I was just like, ‘Oh my God, I have to do that.’”

Chappell, on her main inspiration to use drag in her live performances, BroadwayWorld, September 27, 2023

I think it's very easy to think of the Midwest and South as a monolith. I'm like, 'No, bitch, there are queens everywhere, regardless if you think there are or not.' There are queer people everywhere in these teeny tiny towns who are the same as the bitches on the coasts. They just don't have access to what those girls have. I'm so grateful, because I'm like, no, the flyover states are not just Trump country. There are people desperately wanting to leave like you and me.

Chappell, on drag queens and LGBTQ+ living in conservative regions of the U.S. without access to the queer community, *Paper*, June 4, 2024

The biggest news of the year that fucking hit me like a wave was the fact that Urban Outfitters is selling my vinyl. That's a big deal for 16-year-old me. Like that's crazy! But everything else I'm just like, yeah, whatever.

Chappell, on her biggest success as an artist, *Vanity Fair*, September 18, 2023

The songs are a fairytale version of what happened in real life. With 'Pink Pony Club' I was inspired by a gay club, but I'd never danced on stage at a club. Same with 'Naked in Manhattan' and 'Red Wine Supernova'. I hadn't even kissed a girl or dated a girl when I wrote those songs.

”

Chappell, on her songs being enhanced retellings of events in her life, *Vanity Fair*, September 18, 2023

CHAPTER THREE

IT'S A FEMININOMENON

Chappell Roan isn't just making music – she's making a statement.

With lyrics that reclaim power, challenge expectations and celebrate self-worth, she's a fearless voice in modern pop, fighting for all. Whether she's advocating for feminism, dressing in drag or tackling mental health struggles, her music is raw, honest and wrapped in glitter.

Vulnerable yet defiant, playful yet profound – she reminds us that strength comes in many forms, including platform heels and a killer chorus.

My name is Chappell Roan. I'm your favourite artist's favourite artist. I'm your dream girls, dream girl.

Chappell, opening the now-iconic performance at Coachella Festival 2023*, which was, perhaps, the moment the singer-songwriter truly arrived as a femininomenon, April 2023

** Her hour-long afternoon set was broadcast live on YouTube and gained more than 10 million viewers.*

'Femininomenon' – I open the record with it. If you're not cool with this song, then you're probably not going to like the rest of it.

Chappell, on "Femininomenon", the song that encapsulates everything about Chappell Roan, *Dork*, December 21, 2023

In my artistry, drag fuels everything. Drag is camp and camp is the most fun thing in the world, and that is what I want my project to feel like. Drag has always been a part of society, whether or not people know it. It's been around for so long. I love that it's becoming mainstream. It's such a strange time, but also amazing because drag is blossoming faster than it ever has.

Chappell, on her passion for drag and the importance of it in her act, *Atwood Magazine*, August 26, 2024

I wrote this fucking song, 'Femininomenon' because I can't ever say the actual word femininity. I hated it. I just rejected femininity. So now my whole persona is just me trying to honour that version of myself that I was never allowed to be.

Chappell, on using her onstage drag persona to reject femininity, *Paper*, June 4, 2024

I would say rhinestone, explosive, innovative, bold and feminist.

Chappell, when asked, "In just five words, how would you describe the incredible artist known as Chappell Roan?" interview with Austin Ashburn, February 15, 2023

I have three local drag artists open for me every night where I highly encourage the audience to tip their local girls. We also, as we grow, want to grow the payment of the queens. Also, a portion of every ticket goes to 'For The Gworls' – a black trans charity. We are continuing that since the first tour, and I want to do that for the rest of my career. I think it's so important to give back to the community that gives me so much.

Chappell, on giving back to the trans and drag community while on her Midwest Princess tour 2024, *Atwood Magazine*, August 26, 2024

"

I'm very turned off by celebrity. Some girls have been in this so long that they're used to that, but I'm not that girl. I'm not gonna be a sweetie pie to a man who's telling me to shut the fuck up.

"

Chappell, on male toxic behaviour and being harassed publicly as a celebrity, *The Guardian*, September 20, 2024

What we really need is a femininomenon!

Chappell, on starting a "femininomenonal" feminist movement of her own making, *The Guardian*, September 20, 2024

We will overcome hate. We always do. I will continue doing drag. We will continue this, this is not stopping.

Chappell, on America's southern state "Drag Panic", an unconstitutional ban on drag acts, that began to spread in the U.S. in summer 2023, *Teen Vogue*, March 9, 2023

To grow into the queer girl that I am today, I obviously had to stop dating men who were not it. I had to stop settling for losers and start dating women and getting rid of that shame. I have a girlfriend now, but it's taken baby steps to get to a confident drag queen version of myself.

”

Chappell, on dating a girl, and struggling with her sexuality due to her upbringing, *Salt Lake* magazine, August 29, 2024

This industry fucking thrives on mental illness, burnout, overworking yourself, overextending yourself, not sleeping. You get bigger the more unhealthy you are. Isn't that so fucked up?

Chappell, on the exploitative elements of the modern music industry that feeds on manic self-compulsion, *The Face*, September 16, 2024

Chappell's a drag-queen version of me because she's very larger-than-life. Kind of tacky, not afraid to say really lewd things. That version of me is really fun to play, but it's very exhausting.

99

Chappell, on her drag persona, *Vanity Fair*, September 18, 2023

Bipolar disorder is one of the hardest to treat because you just don't know what's gonna make you feel better. It took me two years to find the right medications but it's so hard with this job because there's no like clocking in and out. I worked at a donut shop for a long time and I loved it because I would just leave work and I would just go watch TV and it was great. But I feel like this is just really hard to take a step away from, especially on tour.

Chappell, on her bipolar disorder diagnosis in 2018, aged 22, after years of struggling with her mental health, *Vanity Fair*, September 18, 2023

I didn't see myself as queer* growing up at all. So that was one hump I had to go over. The other hump was loving myself, feeling confident in my body and loving my music. All three of those things were non-existent. There were so many things that I had to get over that I just deemed impossible for myself, and I think a lot of it came from my community that I grew up in, just not really supporting women in the way that helped women grow out of what served men. I felt that I was only meant to be a mother or a wife and a loyal woman of God, and if I wasn't those things then I was nothing.

Chappell, on the conservative community she grew up part of, *Salt Lake* magazine, August 29, 2024

** Chappell realized she was gay in seventh grade, around age 12–13.*

I have bare feet. I'm not wearing shoes at the outdoor venue today. Did not brush my hair. I'm in pyjamas, free bleeding through my pants.

”

Chappell, on her outfit offstage when not in her drag character, *Paper*, June 4, 2024

"By doing inner child work with my therapist, that's how I got to this conclusion that I needed to be a tacky pop star. I had to let go of the adult in me that thought, 'I need to be so sophisticated and serious and so good at everything or else I'm not good enough.' Also, I'm really attracted to sparkly things and cheetah print."

Chappell, on her personal breakthroughs with her psychotherapist, *Vanity Fair*, September 18, 2023

All I want in life is to feel like a good person, because I felt like such a bad person my whole life – the worst kid in the family, always so out of control and angry. It's been really hard to forgive my parents for not knowing how to handle that correctly and myself, for going through puberty unmedicated and refusing to believe I was anxious or depressed.

Chappell, on her emotional and mental state during her childhood, *The Face*, September 16, 2024

Lady Gaga and Miley Cyrus – what's most inspiring about these two artists is the audacity that they have. They always have the audacity to show up in a meat dress, the audacity to be sexy and have a foam finger, the audacity to perform the way they do is just like what's inspiring to me. It's very feminist. It's just super empowering. I think that's what I love about them.

”

Chappell, on two of her biggest inspirations – Miley Cyrus and Lady Gaga, BroadwayWorld, September 27, 2023

No one is going to take me seriously whenever I release my serious songs because I burn that bridge with my FUCKING! TIKTOK!

”

Chappell, on her TikTok account, which includes her rants about the music industry, discussing her bipolar behaviour, the boundaries of her fans and dating in L.A., *The Face*, September 16, 2024

Being Chappell has really allowed me to explore parts of myself that I wouldn't have if I hadn't chosen this specific path. I could be really brash and really loud and really dressed however I wanted to and almost made it on purpose a drag version of myself so I can be whatever I want.

”

Chappell, on why she chose a drag queen as her alter-ego pop persona, *Vanity Fair*, September 18, 2023

We want liberty, justice and freedom for all. When you do that, that's when I'll come.

Chappell, in a speech made live onstage at the Governor's Ball festival in New York, June 2024, discussing the invitation to perform at a White House Pride event earlier that month that she famously declined.

Chappell Roan is a drag queen version of myself. She's how I deal with this career. It helps me compartmentalize that this is me at work and then this is me not at work. I myself am the brand, my face is the logo, all of that, so it helps when I dress up like a drag queen – I'm in drag and I'm at work and I feel free when I'm that version of myself and more confident and happy on stage.

Chappell, on Chappell Roan as a drag queen version of herself, The Forty-Five, January 18, 2024

When I realized that I should dedicate my career to honouring the childhood I never got, I got big quick. Now, I am the girl who does the Britney routine. I am the girl who plays dress-up. I'm making up for that time.

Chappell, on living out her childhood fantasies she had to repress during childhood, *The Face*, September 16, 2024

I'm very inspired by drag in every aspect. It has really inspired my Chappell project with styling, makeup, performance, music video, the energy around the entire show and the writing is campiness. It's the forefront of the project and the identity. I think that it's the forefront of drag, campiness, over the top, supposed to be fun and dramatic.

Chappell, on the importance of drag in Chappell's show, and personality, Crucial Rhythm, September 12, 2023

If I had to give my younger self advice I would say follow your gut and that you're cool. I always told myself I wish I was cooler, prettier, smarter. But now I would tell her that you are enough exactly how you are in every aspect.

Chappell, on what advice she would give her teenage self, Crucial Rhythm, September 12, 2023

"I hope I look back at this time and still stand behind all the no's that I've said, because I say no to pretty much everything right now. I don't want to fucking go back into the mental hospital because I don't know how to handle my emotions. I hope I don't look back and I'm like, 'Damn, if I just would've sucked it up and pushed a little harder.' I don't think I will, but I'm always scared of that."

Chappell, on sacrificing massive opportunities for the sake of her mental health, *Interview*, August 19, 2024

The album represents me as a person. I'm very sensitive. I'm definitely romantic. That comes with high highs and low lows. That's where the album title *The Rise and Fall of a Midwest Princess* comes into play. The songs capture that feeling. It showcases how I'm three-dimensional.

Chappell, on her album *The Rise and Fall of a Midwest Princess*, *Dork*, December 21, 2023

I started gaining a lot of followers when I was being really insane on TikTok. I wasn't sleeping. I was on the incorrect meds. I had the energy and the delusion and realized that the app is fuelled off of mental illness.

Chappell, on social media feeding off negative mental health, *Independent*, September 12, 2024

CHAPTER FOUR

SUPER GRAPHIC ULTRA-MODERN GIRL

Brash. Tacky. Rude. Loud. Lewd.

Chappell Roan is proudly all of these things. But, underneath all the makeup, Chappell is also a whole lot more.

She is a joy-filled agent of essential change for the LGBTQ+ community and a breath of fresh air for the homogenized pop industry machine.

She is, quite simply, the very modern model of a major modern icon…

I went to the gay club once and it was so impactful, like magic. It was the opposite of everything I was taught.

Chappell Roan, on her first experience at a gay club, *The Guardian*, December 29, 2023

I can't read my DMs anymore, because I cry so much. People send messages like, 'Whatever you're doing, it helped me.' No award or money can be exchanged for that compliment. I don't care about anything else, except giving space to people to be free. Because that's what I needed so bad: Freedom.

”

Chappell, on the influence and inspiration she gives her fans to be free to live their own truths, *The Face*, September 16, 2024

The Rise and Fall of a Midwest Princess

1. "Femininomenon"
2. "Red Wine Supernova"
3. "After Midnight"
4. "Coffee"
5. "Casual"
6. "Super Graphic Ultra-Modern Girl"
7. "HOT TO GO!"
8. "My Kink Is Karma"
9. "Picture You"
10. "Kaleidoscope"
11. "Pink Pony Club"
12. "Naked In Manhattan"
13. "California"
14. "Guilty Pleasure"

I got signed a year after *Ultraviolence* came out in 2014. That's how long I've been here. That's how many Lana Del Rey albums are in between. I've been here the whole time!

Chappell, on her 10-year career as "overnight sensation" and having only released one studio album, *The Face*, September 16, 2024

I know this sounds cocky, but I'm not that surprised people like the album… because it's really good.

”

Chappell, on her album *The Rise and Fall of a Midwest Princess*, *Dork*, December 21, 2023

The people we're performing for in Midwest and Southern states, the money they used to buy tickets to see us was made at a job where they're afraid of acting gay. That's how severe it is.

Chappell, on the difficulty of being part of the LGBTQ+ community in America's Bible Belt states, *Paper*, June 4, 2024

I was so picky when I got signed again. I met with nine labels and I went in with the attitude of, 'The only thing I need right now is money.' So if you don't give me this, this and this, I'm just not going to sign with you because I can keep going on my own. I was very picky and I had a fuck ton of leverage.

Chappell, on choosing her record label home after the experience of being dropped by Atlantic Records in 2020, *NME*, June 21, 2023

“Part of me hopes I never have a hit again because then no one will ever expect anything from me again.”

Chappell, on her anxieties surrounding having to repeat success, *Rolling Stone*, September 10, 2024

Do people know when they dress up for football games and paint their faces and do their hair crazy, that's drag? I don't think most people know what a drag show is so I bet they would have a lot of fun. I'm just like, you should come!

Chappell, on people who criticize drag, and drag queens, without knowing what it really is, *Salt Lake* magazine, August 29, 2024

There was no queer representation. I didn't know a single out lesbian girl, gay girl, bi girl, nothing. There were a couple of gay boys in my school who were out and they got terrorized, slurred, threatened. It was a sin to them. I saw what would happen if you came out.

Chappell, on being gay in a small U.S. conservative and religious town, *Salt Lake* magazine, August 29, 2024

My career doesn't mean anything more now that I have a charting album and song. A chart is so fleeting. Everyone leaves the charts.

”

Chappell, on suddenly having chart success in 2024, after 10 years, and it not meaning as much as it used to, *Interview*, August 19, 2024

Chappell released her debut album on Island Records on September 22, 2023. It received great acclaim amongst her growing number of fans, or Chappies.

A slow-burn sleeper hit, the album reached the U.S. Billboard Top Ten nine months later, in June 2024, following the success of the single "HOT TO GO!".

The album earned Chappell her first Grammy Award nominations and first Grammy win at the 67th annual ceremony in 2025, making her one of 12 artists in history to have earned Grammy nominations in all of the "Big Four" categories for their debut studio album, including Album of the Year, Record of the Year, Song of the Year and Best New Artist.

I am very introverted. I love being alone. I love playing video games by myself. My favourite thing to do is get really high and play Fortnite or Mario.

Chappell, on what she does when she's not being Chappell, *Vanity Fair*, September 18, 2023

'Super Graphic Ultra Modern Girl' – I literally just wrote it to do poppers to. It was written for the gays.

Chappell, on songwriting camps, *NME*, June 21, 2023

I'm not good at hot, but I am good at scary.

Chappell, on her drag queen stage costumer aesthetic, *The Face*, September 16, 2024

"I'm the pop star of Goodwill. I'm a thrift store pop star. I'm a DIY queen, know what I mean?"

Chappell, defining Chappell, *Rolling Stone*, October 27, 2022

“

I was so desperate to feel understood. I pushed down the gay part of myself so deep because I was like, that can’t possibly be me.

”

Chappell, on repressing her sexuality during her religious Southern childhood, *The Guardian*, September 20, 2024

I just want to create a fun place for people – especially queer people – to feel safe, dress up, and know that they’re not gonna be judged.

”

Chappell, on her ultimate ambition for her live performances and world tours, February 15, 2023

I was signed for five years to Atlantic Records when I started making music, and then I was dropped in 2020 like everyone was. I was working at a donut shop. No money. I had moved back in with my parents during the pandemic because I couldn't get a job in L.A.

Chappell, on being released from her long-term Atlantic Records contract and moving back home to Missouri for a year, *Paper*, June 4, 2024

I feel more love than I ever have in my life. I also feel the most unsafe I have ever felt in my life. There is a part of myself that I save just for my project and all of you. There is a part of myself that is just for me, and I don't want that taken away from me.

”

Chappell, in an online message to her "super fans" calling out their toxic behaviour, Instagram, August 23, 2024

Your Favourite Artist's Favourite Artist

In the past 12 months, Chappell's praises have been sung by just about everyone!

"I've been just as obsessed with her as everyone has."

Sabrina Carpenter
Rolling Stone, June 2024

"She is kind, innocent, and wonderful. She is not 'Chappell Roan' offstage – a bit like me. She is one of those people who I felt like I have known for a long time. I am very protective of her."

Elton John
Rolling Stone, September 10, 2024

"Chappell Roan is talented and interesting."

Beyoncé
GQ, September 2024

"She is spectacular, and it turns out, she's not just got one song. She's got, like, seven fucking brilliant songs. I think she's absolutely amazing."

Adele

Live on stage, Munich's Messe München, August 2024

"I absolutely adore her. I think she is one of the most singular, inspiring, powerful artists I've ever had the pleasure of meeting, and I'm so excited because she's gonna sing one of my favourite songs of all time."

Olivia Rodrigo

Live on stage in Los Angeles, introducing Chappell, August 2024

I probably have one of the best deals ever in modern music because I was like: 'Fuck you guys, give me what I want or I'm going to do this myself.' Now I can be like: 'Look at the numbers, bitch.'

”

Chappell Roan, on her label deal with Island Records, *The Face*, September 26, 2024

Before I moved to West Hollywood, I had really never even seen a drag queen before. I was 18. But when I went to Disney World when I was 7 and I saw Princess Jasmine, it's no different than me watching a drag show now. I'm in such awe of the makeup, the hair, the outfit, the dancing, the songs. It's just magical to me, and I just think it's the funniest thing ever to watch a drag show.

Chappell, on when she first experienced drag and drag queens, *Salt Lake* magazine, August 29, 2024

If I hear Lady Gaga or Nicki Minaj on a playlist, it instantly takes me to this place of 'Yeah, party!' And that's the place I want to take people to as well. I want to give them that emotion of 'We're here, bitch, we're here and we're queer.'

”

Chappell, when asked "What do you want people to think when they hear the name Chappell Roan?", *NME*, June 21, 2023

Originally, I thought I was gonna be an actress and singing could be a way for me to get a foot in the door. I wasn't, like, a savant at music or anything. But then when I was about 15 or 16, I went to songwriting camps – like, summer art camps where I met a lot of kids like me. And that was really helpful. I put a song out, 'Die Young', that I actually wrote at a summer camp. And that's what ended up getting me signed. I was 17 and still in high school – I was a literal minor. It's so crazy, but thank God for the summer camps because they got me where I am today.

Chappell, on the significance of songwriting camps to awaken her writing process, *NME*, June 21, 2023

I am very adamant about giving back to the queer community, and that is what I encourage other artists to do, whether they're queer or not: just giving back to the community that supports them so much, whether that be by lowering ticket prices to what they can, or lowering merch prices to what they can, or donating a portion of every ticket or doing charity events. Because no one's going to stand up for queer people. It's got to be us. We have to support each other.

Chappell, on giving back to the communities that support her, *Salt Lake* magazine, August 29, 2024

I'm so focused on hitting midwestern markets that a lot of artists don't hit. There are so many queer teens and young people that really need this... because I know I did.

Chappell, on focusing on visiting America's Midwest during her tour, BroadwayWorld, September 27, 2023

Her First Song

In August 2017, Chappell released her debut single, "Good Hurt", as Chappell Roan.

Her debut EP, *School Nights*, was released a month later.

When I sing, I want people to feel every emotion. I hope they get a better understanding of me as a human being and not just as a singer. I want you to know who I am. All of my songs come directly from my personal experiences. 'Good Hurt' happens to come from a time when I was in a relationship, but wanted a different person who was toxic for me. The song is about me wanting something that I know is not good for me.

Chappell, on the meaning of her very first song, *Interview* magazine, August 2017

"I feel like I did miss out on having friends. I didn't have a lot of friends and I feel like I would've made more. That's why I wish I would've gone to college, just because I would have so many friends. But now I have a ton and it's great."

Chappell, on not being diagnosed as bipolar until much later in life, and missing out on having more friends as a result, *Vanity Fair*, September 18, 2023

I was upset about my album not moving. I felt stuck and like no one was paying attention to me. Daniel Nigro was just looking at me and said, 'You are going to run your career into the fucking ground if you don't start doing shit on your own.'

Chappell, on producer Daniel Nigro halting work with Chappell to work on Olivia Rodrigo's *Sour*, and taking her destiny into her own hands, *Rolling Stone*, October 27, 2022

I have so many issues with our government in every way. There are so many things that I would want to change. We cannot have cis people making decisions for trans people, period.

Chappell, on the issue of trans rights at the 2024 U.S. Election, *The Guardian*, September 20, 2024

I love a pure white face. I started to do that, because that's what the country boys called gay people in my hometown. Clowns. I was just like, 'Bitch, I'll show you a clown, if you want to see a clown! So I started doing that and also referencing the girls in the '20s with blue eyeshadow, a big red lip and glitter – my faves.

Chappell, on the origin of her drag look and style, and growing up in Missouri, *Paper*, June 4, 2024

That's the beauty of drag, and then making it a pop persona that is a drag queen. It's like, I'm going out onstage in a frickin' dress made out of Wrangler pants. I can do that.

Chappell, on the creative fashion freedom of her drag-pop persona, *Paper*, June 4, 2024

I can only do what I'm best at, which is writing and singing music. If there's an expectation to act as a spokesperson for queer people any expectation is not going to be met because I'm not that girl – one person cannot speak for an entire community. And don't expect a popstar to speak for you!

Chappell, on not being a spokesperson for the entire gay community, Brown University Interviews, November 15, 2023

What's so amazing is to be in parts of the U.S. and just knowing the governor of the state hates gay people but the people at my shows don't give a fuck and they are just living their best life! Florida has a Don't Say Gay law. But at my show the whole crowd was just chanting 'Gay, gay, gay!' over and over again. It was just like so empowering to see there are queer kids everywhere and all of them are willing to fight for their rights.

Chappell, on empowering her audience at her live shows, The Forty-Five, January 18, 2024

I love anthemic pop. I go in to the studio every time like, how do we make the biggest, funniest song ever?

Chappell, on her signature sound, *Teen Vogue*, March 9, 2023

CHAPTER FIVE

HOT TO GO-GO-GO!

Armed with as many solid gold bangers as her peers Sabrina Carpenter, Olivia Rodrigo and Billie Eilish, it's little wonder that Chappell's worldwide success has followed hot on the heels of her hit song "HOT TO GO!", a dollop of pop so delicious it makes you wonder what else she has hidden up her sleeves…

"

Genuinely, I was stressing when 'HOT TO GO!' came out because I was scared that people were not going to take me seriously as a writer. Because that song – there's not a song of depth. Like 'Femininomenon' – I just remember kicking myself, saying 'That is such a stupid song!'

"

Chappell, on the pop simplicity of "HOT TO GO!" and "Femininomenon", *Variety*, November 11, 2024

Tiny Desk

1. "Casual"
2. "Pink Pony Club"
3. "Picture You"
4. "California"
5. "Red Wine Supernova"

Now regarded as one of the best Tiny Desk performances ever recorded for the online concert series "NPR's Tiny Desk", Chappell's 23-minute long set, performed on March 21, 2024, solidified her status as America's brightest rising star and became a huge milestone moment in a year of milestone moments.

Her seven-strong live band, all dressed in pink, killed it too. The performance was so amazing it increased her Spotify monthly listeners count by 500 per cent! Check it out on YouTube now!

“

I’ve never given a fuck about the charts or being on the radio, but it’s so crazy how industry people are taking me more seriously than before. I’m like, ‘I’ve been doing this the whole time, bitch.’

”

Chappell, on her “overnight” 10-year rise to fame, and the music industry’s approach to her success, *Interview*, August 19, 2024

I saw the Queen movie with Rami Malek (*Bohemian Rhapsody*) and the whole crowd was doing this chanting. I was like, how do I make the crowd do that?

Chappell, on the inspiration behind "HOT TO GO!"*,
Teen Vogue, March 9, 2023

** Chappell wrote the song two weeks before the start of her 2023 tour. It became an instant live hit, and every night Chappell guides the audience to learn the cheer dance – though most fans have mastered it now!*

I just wanted to be Hannah Montana. That's what I liked when I was little.

Chappell, on Miley Cyrus' famous alter ego, Hannah Montana, *People*, July 17, 2024

I've allowed myself to write songs that maybe some would say is tacky, but actually, I just think it's camp. It's been a growing process of allowing myself to just have fun. I think the music industry, especially in the U.S., is very serious, and they don't want you to have fun.

Chappell, on bringing the fun back to American pop music, *Dork*, December 21, 2023

What's so infuriating is how people are just now taking me seriously. Like, 'You know what, bitch? I've been doing this shit for a long time and you're just now catching up.'

Chappell, on the media all of a sudden being interested in Chappell and her music, *Rolling Stone*, September 10, 2024

People think I'm complaining about my success. I'm complaining about being abused.

Chappell, on the unwarranted abuse and harassment she receives as a celebrity, *The Guardian*, September 20, 2024

I just need to capture the British soccer people. I need the World Cup to get on board with 'HOT TO GO!' and then I'm fucking set forever.

Chappell, on brand deals, and saying no to anything that doesn't feel "100 per cent right", *Rolling Stone*, September 10, 2024

It's a cheer song, so there's a dance attached to it. It's like 'Y.M.C.A.' but gayer.

Chappell, on her big hit song "HOT TO GO!", and its accompanying cheer squad dance, February 15, 2023

My career has worked because I've done it my way, and I've not compromised morals and time. I have not succumbed to the pressure. Like, 'Bitch! I'm not doing a brand deal if it doesn't feel right. I don't care how much you're paying me.' That's why I can sleep at night.

Chappell, on never compromising on her career, *Interview*, August 19, 2024

As I grow the project grows with me and as I experience more outrageous things in my life the songs get more and more outrageous. As long as I'm changing, the music will change with me. That's why 'HOT TO GO!' is so different from 'Pink Pony Club', cause those were written years apart.

Chappell, on her evolution and growth as an artist, Crucial Rhythm, September 12, 2023

It is nice to have the pop-star treatment. To be like, 'I would love to go see Alanis Morissette and Joan Jett. They want me to sit in a suite? Okaaaaay!' There is a lot of fun to be had.

Chappell, on the upsides to being famous and a celebrity, *The Guardian*, September 20, 2024

It's been amazing to do bigger shows, and open for Olivia Rodrigo. Everything right now is truly icing on the cake… but I feel like I peaked a couple of years ago.

Chappell, on touring with Olivia Rodrigo, and reaching a peak of success she was comfortable with, *Interview*, August 19, 2024

I'm really glad the persona that I have, the drag version, is still very much me.

Chappell, on remaining true to herself while in drag, *Interview*, August 19, 2024

1. "Femininomenon"
2. "Naked in Manhattan"
3. "Super Graphic Ultra-Modern Girl"
4. "HOT TO GO!"
5. "After Midnight"
6. "Barracuda"
7. "Casual"
8. "The Subway"
9. "Red Wine Supernova"
10. "Good Luck, Babe!"
11. "My Kink Is Karma"
12. "Pink Pony Club"

The setlist to Chappell's largest gig (so far!) at Austin's City Limits Festival, Zilker Park, Austin, Texas, U.S., on October 6, 2024. More than 80,000 fans were there for Chappell, one of the largest audiences the festival has ever attracted!

"

In the past eight weeks, my entire life has changed. It's been really emotional because I'm not just singing pop music, it's automatically political because I'm gay. The biggest thing has been getting recognized, and just feeling not myself. I've never given a fuck about the charts or being on the radio, but it's so crazy how industry people are taking me more seriously than before.

"

Chappell Roan, on her "overnight" fame found in summer 2024 and announcing her sexuality, *Interview*, August 19, 2024

I've been trained how to act, but it's the most stressful thing in the world to me. I would rather get arrested.

Chappell, on acting, and being an actor, *Interview*, August 19, 2024

I would not be the Midwest Princess I am today if I had been around art kids. I look at my life and I think, 'Everything was exactly as it should have been.'

Chappell, on her conservative upbringing being responsible for her success, not in spite of, *Interview*, August 19, 2024

“

I love vegetable pizza the most, but I can’t possibly miss the opportunity to call my own pizza Chappellroanie Pepperoni. It’s just too perfect.

”

Chappell, on her dream pizza, I Dream of Vinyl, May 7, 2020

"The album is the storyline of a girl who moved from a small conservative town to a city and had an awakening of this world she never knew existed. Which includes queerness, heartbreak, falling in love, the city and clubs – and it's the world of Chappell Roan."

Chappell, on the concept narrative of *The Rise and Fall of a Midwest Princess*, *Teen Vogue*, March 9, 2023

I feel like I'm just being my 10-year-old self. This whole project is to honour my 10-year-old self.

Chappell Roan, on finally being her own true self, *Paper*, June 4, 2024

They were immediately, immediately supportive. Immediately. It's been so amazing, because I'm very scared and confused.

”

Chappell, on the support of her "little pop star girlies", such as Lady Gaga, Charli XCX, Lorde and Sabrina Carpenter, helping her navigate through overwhelming sudden success, *The Face*, September 16, 2024

I wanted a cheer song. So literally what I did was Google classic cheerleading cheers. I wanted to be a cheerleader so bad because I always thought they were just so cool and so hot. They were just so sassy at my school. I never had the confidence to try out because I just thought I didn't belong. And so it's another dream-come-true vibes. It follows the same path as how my other songs are like dreams come true.

Chappell, on "HOT TO GO!", her biggest hit song to date, *Vanity Fair*, September 18, 2023

It's my favourite part of life, having a crush on someone. It's the best thing ever when you are at the beginning of a relationship and talking on FaceTime for eight hours a day. I'm a relationship girl. I've never dated someone less than a year. So I always cherish the honeymoon phase.

Chappell, on the start of a new relationship, and falling in love, *Interview*, August 19, 2024

I released 'Pink Pony Club' in April 2020. It was a very dark time when it came out. No one could party, and it was West Hollywood's anthem! It's for going out and queerness, and it was just so sad that I couldn't perform it. It was on the shelf for two years because concerts won't open, you know? It was a bummer, but I know it helped a lot of people through the pandemic. Now, we're here! Thank God!

Chappell, on the original release "Pink Pony Club" as a single via Atlantic Records in 2020, during the pandemic, and subsequent single release in 2022 on Island Records, Pop Crave, February 15, 2023

"For the past 10 years I've been going nonstop to build my project and it's come to the point that I need to draw lines and set boundaries. I've been in too many nonconsensual physical and social interactions. I chose this career path because I love music and art and honouring my inner child, I do not accept harassment of any kind because I chose this path, nor do I deserve it. Please stop touching me. Please stop being weird to my family and friends. Please stop assuming things about me."

Chappell, on her "fans" and critics getting too close for comfort, Instagram, August 23, 2024

“

We’re both going through something so fucking hard… she just feels like everything is flying, and she’s just barely hanging on. It was just good to know someone else feels that way.

”

Chappell, on Sabrina Carpenter, another rising young female artist in America, *Rolling Stone*, September 10, 2024

My whole persona is just me trying to honour that version of myself that I was never allowed to be.

Chappell, on no longer having to repress her childhood fantasies, and channelling them through her drag persona, *Paper*, June 4, 2024

With more than 42 million monthly listeners on Spotify and more than three billion total streams on the platform to date, Chappell Roan is now one of the most streamed female artists – ever!

Her most popular song on the platform is "Good Luck, Babe!", with more than one billion streams. Hot on its heels is "HOT TO GO!", with more than half a billion!

With 'HOT TO GO!' and 'Femininomenon', those songs were difficult for me to put out because of how hateful people are. Some people just don't get the joke and don't have fun with music. They don't get the camp of it all, that it's supposed to be silly, and it's not necessarily supposed to feel like serious music, you know?

Chappell, on making her music as silly and fun as possible – on purpose, BroadwayWorld, September 27, 2023

I just love performing. I feel very myself on stage. I feel like that's what I was put on this Earth for – to throw fun parties.

Chappell, on her live performances, *Salt Lake* magazine, August 29, 2024

I embrace the success of my music, the love I feel, and the gratitude I have. What I do not accept are creepy people, being touched, and being followed.

Chappell, on the toxic behaviour of her "super fans", Instagram, August 23, 2024

Fame is just abusive: Stalking, talking shit online, people who won't leave you alone, yelling at you in public – is the vibe of an abusive ex-husband.

Chappell, on stalkers, trolls, harassers and paparazzi, *The Face*, September 16, 2024

They're so into the Chappell Roan world from a very surface-level perspective, 'cause they won't go deeper because they think it's a lot. My grandma literally said it's a little too much, which I understand. The lyrics are really a lot to listen to. But they were so down to learn it. They're just really proud of me and they always have been.

”

Chappell, on her supportive parents and family, Dwight and Kara Amstutz, *Vanity Fair*, September 18, 2023

I get told by a lot of people that my album is their getting ready to go out music, but I think because the songs are so narrative that it could be listened to in a small house party or driving on a road trip or just having fun with your friends. I think craft night is fun to listen to or fun girly slumber parties!

Chappell, on the perfect environment to listen to her debut album, Crucial Rhythm, September 12, 2023

I'm just trying to balance both me as Kayleigh and Chappell. It's difficult sometimes because it's so emotional. Obviously the emotions come from me as a human and not as a character.

Chappell, on balancing her life between being Kayleigh and being Chappell, BroadwayWorld, September 27, 2023